Advanced Multiplication

H.S. Lawrence

Illustration by
Kathy Kifer

Special thanks to:
Holly Dye, Derrick Hoffman, Jane Tory, Carrie Hernandez,
Caroline Jeanbart, Susan Rovetta, and Cecily Cleveland

Published by
Garlic Press
100 Hillview Lane #2
Eugene, OR 97401

ISBN 0-931993-62-8
Order Number GP-062

Overview: Math and Animal Science

The Puzzles and Practice Series builds basic **math skills** and acquaints students with **animal science**. The Series is also designed to challenge skills associated with following directions, simple logic, visual discrimination (all puzzle assembly skills), and motor skills (cutting and pasting).

Practice Pages illustrate math skills step-by-step, then provide extended practice. **Puzzle Pages** contain twelve-piece puzzles that when assembled reveal a fascinating animal. This book in the Series features Polar Animals.

Polar Animals Reference Cards, found on the last three pages of this book, provide further information for students. In addition, for parents and teachers, the inside front cover provides **background information** on Polar Animals.

Helping Teachers and Parents

There are two pages for each of the twelve lessons- a Practice Page and a Puzzle Page. Each page can be used independently; however, the Puzzles and Practice Series has incorporated a special feature that encourages the use of both pages at one time.

Special Feature - If you hold a *Puzzle Page* up to the light, you will see the same problems showing in the center of the puzzle pieces (actually showing through from the *Practice Page*) that are to the left of the puzzle pieces on the Puzzle Page. This feature is useful so a student will not lose the potential for the answer after he or she has cut out the puzzle piece. This feature is also useful if a student does not follow directions and cuts out all puzzle pieces at one time.

Table of Contents

$$
15 \quad \rightarrow \quad
\overset{2}{1}5 \quad \rightarrow \quad
\overset{2}{1}5 \quad \rightarrow \quad
15
$$

$$
\begin{array}{r} 15 \\ \times\,4 \\ \hline \end{array}
\quad
\begin{array}{r} \mathbf{2} \\ 1\mathbf{5} \\ \times\,\mathbf{4} \\ \hline \mathbf{0} \end{array}
\quad
\begin{array}{r} \mathbf{2} \\ \mathbf{1}5 \\ \times\,\mathbf{4} \\ \hline \mathbf{6}0 \end{array}
\quad
\begin{array}{r} 15 \\ \times\,4 \\ \hline 60 \end{array}
$$

19	24	16	45	14	28	16	37
x 2	x 3	x 4	x 2	x 4	x 3	x 6	x 2
18	49	15	28	23	12	14	25
x 3	x 2	x 5	x 2	x 4	x 7	x 5	x 3
24	17	25	29	17	15	38	27
x 4	x 5	x 2	x 3	x 4	x 6	x 2	x 3
36	19	26	12	47	13	15	26
x 2	x 5	x 3	x 5	x 2	x 7	x 3	x 2

**NAME
NOMBRE** _____

Instructions:

1. Answer <u>all</u> the math problems first.
2. Cut out <u>one</u> puzzle piece at a time.
3. Paste the puzzle piece in the box with the same answer.

Instrucciones:

1. Conteste <u>todos</u> los problemas de matemáticas primero.
2. Recorte <u>una</u> pieza del rompecabezas a la vez.
3. Pegue la pieza del rompecabezas en el recuadro que tiene la misma respuesta.

54	78	92	76
70	45	72	50
96	68	94	75

14
x 5

23
x 4

15
x 5

18
x 3

38
x 2
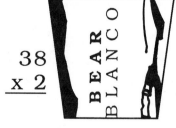

17
x 4

25
x 2

24
x 4

15
x 3
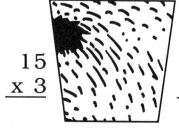

47
x 2

26
x 3

36
x 2

2

$$
\begin{array}{r} 87 \\ \times\ 6 \\ \hline \end{array}
\rightarrow
\begin{array}{r} {}^{4}\\ 87 \\ \times\ \mathbf{6} \\ \hline \mathbf{2} \end{array}
\rightarrow
\begin{array}{r} {}^{4}\\ \mathbf{8}7 \\ \times\ \mathbf{6} \\ \hline \mathbf{5}\mathbf{2}2 \end{array}
\rightarrow
\begin{array}{r} 87 \\ \times\ 6 \\ \hline 522 \end{array}
$$

75	68	83	56	93	47	86	79
x 9	x 2	x 7	x 5	x 8	x 4	x 6	x 3

18	33	85	72	24	65	56	97
x 6	x 8	x 4	x 6	x 9	x 3	x 7	x 9

34	47	62	54	87	63	98	36
x 8	x 7	x 9	x 3	x 5	x 6	x 8	x 4

53	86	68	75	57	79	95	69
x 5	x 9	x 7	x 4	x 2	x 8	x 6	x 3

NAME
NOMBRE _____

Instructions:

1. Answer <u>all</u> the math problems first.
2. Cut out <u>one</u> puzzle piece at a time.
3. Paste the puzzle piece in the box with the same answer.

Instrucciones:

1. Conteste <u>todos</u> los problemas de matemáticas primero.
2. Recorte <u>una</u> pieza del rompecabezas a la vez.
3. Pegue la pieza del rompecabezas en el recuadro que tiene la misma respuesta.

340	570	392	784
558	265	435	272
114	216	476	108

$$\begin{array}{r} 56 \\ \times\ 7 \\ \hline \end{array}$$

$$\begin{array}{r} 24 \\ \times\ 9 \\ \hline \end{array}$$

$$\begin{array}{r} 85 \\ \times\ 4 \\ \hline \end{array}$$

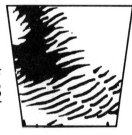
$$\begin{array}{r} 18 \\ \times\ 6 \\ \hline \end{array}$$

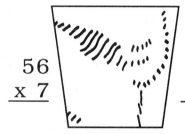
$$\begin{array}{r} 98 \\ \times\ 8 \\ \hline \end{array}$$

$$\begin{array}{r} 87 \\ \times\ 5 \\ \hline \end{array}$$

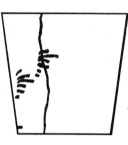
$$\begin{array}{r} 62 \\ \times\ 9 \\ \hline \end{array}$$

$$\begin{array}{r} 34 \\ \times\ 8 \\ \hline \end{array}$$

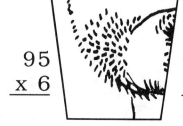
$$\begin{array}{r} 95 \\ \times\ 6 \\ \hline \end{array}$$

$$\begin{array}{r} 57 \\ \times\ 2 \\ \hline \end{array}$$

$$\begin{array}{r} 68 \\ \times\ 7 \\ \hline \end{array}$$

$$\begin{array}{r} 53 \\ \times\ 5 \\ \hline \end{array}$$

4

$$
387 \rightarrow \overset{2}{3}87 \rightarrow \overset{3\,2}{3}87 \rightarrow \overset{3\,2}{3}87 \rightarrow 387
$$

$$
\underline{\times 4} \qquad \underline{\times 4} \qquad \underline{\times 4} \qquad \underline{\times 4} \qquad \underline{\times 4}
$$

$$
\qquad\qquad 8 \qquad\quad 48 \qquad\quad 1548 \qquad 1{,}548
$$

© Garlic Press Eugene, OR

875	699	825	749	954	494	365	573
x 5	x 2	x 4	x 7	x 9	x 6	x 3	x 8

649	757	935	884	766	875	643	267
x 6	x 3	x 9	x 4	x 8	x 2	x 4	x 5

858	583	562	618	879	927	155	936
x 2	x 9	x 6	x 8	x 4	x 6	x 8	x 3

192	736	942	386	535	918	783	647
x 9	x 5	x 7	x 3	x 4	x 9	x 5	x 8

**NAME
NOMBRE** _____

Instructions:

1. **Answer all the math problems first.**
2. **Cut out one puzzle piece at a time.**
3. **Paste the puzzle piece in the box with the same answer.**

Instrucciones:

1. Conteste todos los problemas de matemáticas primero.
2. Recorte una pieza del rompecabezas a la vez.
3. Pegue la pieza del rompecabezas en el recuadro que tiene la misma respuesta.

6,128	**1,240**	**3,372**	**8,415**
3,915	**3,894**	**2,140**	**1,728**
1,716	**6,594**	**2,572**	**3,516**

643
x 4
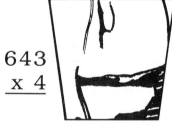

766
x 8

935
x 9

649
x 6

155
x 8

879
x 4

562
x 6

858
x 2

783
x 5

535
x 4

942
x 7

192
x 9

$$
\begin{array}{r} 437 \\ \times\ 8 \\ \hline \end{array}
\rightarrow
\begin{array}{r} \overset{5}{43}7 \\ \times\ \mathbf{8} \\ \hline \mathbf{6} \end{array}
\rightarrow
\begin{array}{r} \overset{2\ 5}{4\mathbf{3}7} \\ \times\ \mathbf{8} \\ \hline \mathbf{9}6 \end{array}
\rightarrow
\begin{array}{r} \overset{2\ 5}{\mathbf{4}37} \\ \times\ \mathbf{8} \\ \hline \mathbf{34}96 \end{array}
\rightarrow
\begin{array}{r} 437 \\ \times\ 8 \\ \hline 3{,}496 \end{array}
$$

© Garlic Press Eugene, OR

723 × 6	224 × 7	348 × 3	963 × 5	577 × 2	393 × 9	948 × 8	865 × 2
468 × 3	579 × 9	365 × 6	947 × 3	132 × 9	954 × 4	396 × 7	694 × 5
375 × 7	746 × 9	347 × 4	992 × 8	245 × 5	853 × 4	724 × 9	158 × 8
934 × 8	596 × 2	458 × 5	817 × 7	956 × 9	683 × 6	827 × 8	649 × 7

NAME
NOMBRE _____

Instructions:

1. Answer <u>all</u> the math problems first.
2. Cut out <u>one</u> puzzle piece at a time.
3. Paste the puzzle piece in the box with the same answer.

Instrucciones:

1. Conteste <u>todos</u> los problemas de matemáticas primero.
2. Recorte <u>una</u> pieza del rompecabezas a la vez.
3. Pegue la pieza del rompecabezas en el recuadro que tiene la misma respuesta.

6,516	2,625	1,188	1,388
2,190	8,604	2,290	1,404
7,472	2,772	1,225	6,616

396
x 7

132
x 9

365
x 6

468
x 3

724
x 9

245
x 5

347
x 4

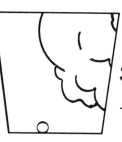

375
x 7

827
x 8

956
x 9

458
x 5

934
x 8

$$
\begin{array}{c}
22 \\
\underline{\times 13}
\end{array}
\rightarrow
\begin{array}{c}
2\mathbf{2} \\
\underline{\times 1\mathbf{3}} \\
\mathbf{6}
\end{array}
\rightarrow
\begin{array}{c}
\mathbf{2}2 \\
\underline{\times 1\mathbf{3}} \\
\mathbf{6}6
\end{array}
\rightarrow
\begin{array}{c}
2\mathbf{2} \\
\underline{\times \mathbf{1}3} \\
66 \\
\mathbf{2}0
\end{array}
\rightarrow
\begin{array}{c}
\mathbf{2}2 \\
\underline{\times \mathbf{1}3} \\
66 \\
\mathbf{2}20
\end{array}
\rightarrow
\begin{array}{c}
22 \\
\underline{\times 13} \\
66 \\
\underline{+220} \\
286
\end{array}
$$

© Garlic Press Eugene, OR

| $\begin{array}{r}21\\ \times 43\end{array}$ | $\begin{array}{r}33\\ \times 22\end{array}$ | $\begin{array}{r}11\\ \times 79\end{array}$ | $\begin{array}{r}23\\ \times 22\end{array}$ | $\begin{array}{r}75\\ \times 11\end{array}$ | $\begin{array}{r}31\\ \times 23\end{array}$ | $\begin{array}{r}12\\ \times 44\end{array}$ | $\begin{array}{r}76\\ \times 11\end{array}$ |

| $\begin{array}{r}21\\ \times 34\end{array}$ | $\begin{array}{r}11\\ \times 83\end{array}$ | $\begin{array}{r}42\\ \times 12\end{array}$ | $\begin{array}{r}22\\ \times 44\end{array}$ | $\begin{array}{r}56\\ \times 11\end{array}$ | $\begin{array}{r}41\\ \times 22\end{array}$ | $\begin{array}{r}11\\ \times 74\end{array}$ | $\begin{array}{r}23\\ \times 23\end{array}$ |

| $\begin{array}{r}22\\ \times 14\end{array}$ | $\begin{array}{r}13\\ \times 32\end{array}$ | $\begin{array}{r}69\\ \times 11\end{array}$ | $\begin{array}{r}21\\ \times 44\end{array}$ | $\begin{array}{r}34\\ \times 12\end{array}$ | $\begin{array}{r}11\\ \times 85\end{array}$ | $\begin{array}{r}32\\ \times 23\end{array}$ | $\begin{array}{r}47\\ \times 11\end{array}$ |

| $\begin{array}{r}43\\ \times 22\end{array}$ | $\begin{array}{r}11\\ \times 67\end{array}$ | $\begin{array}{r}32\\ \times 22\end{array}$ | $\begin{array}{r}12\\ \times 43\end{array}$ | $\begin{array}{r}11\\ \times 78\end{array}$ | $\begin{array}{r}65\\ \times 11\end{array}$ | $\begin{array}{r}13\\ \times 33\end{array}$ | $\begin{array}{r}22\\ \times 34\end{array}$ |

NAME
NOMBRE _____

Instructions:

1. **Answer all the math problems first.**
2. **Cut out one puzzle piece at a time.**
3. **Paste the puzzle piece in the box with the same answer.**

Instrucciones:

1. Conteste todos los problemas de matemáticas primero.
2. Recorte una pieza del rompecabezas a la vez.
3. Pegue la pieza del rompecabezas en el recuadro que tiene la misma respuesta.

714	308	759	814
429	616	946	408
736	858	504	704

11
x 74

56
x 11

42
x 12

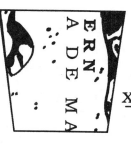

21
x 34

32
x 23

34
x 12

69
x 11

22
x 14

13
x 33

11
x 78

32
x 22

43
x 22

10

© Garlic Press
Eugene, OR

$$
\begin{array}{c}
62 \\
\times 52 \\
\end{array}
\rightarrow
\begin{array}{c}
6\mathbf{2} \\
\times 5\mathbf{2} \\
\hline
\mathbf{4} \\
\end{array}
\rightarrow
\begin{array}{c}
\mathbf{6}2 \\
\times 5\mathbf{2} \\
\hline
\mathbf{12}4 \\
\end{array}
\rightarrow
\begin{array}{c}
\overset{1}{6}2 \\
\times \mathbf{52} \\
\hline
124 \\
\mathbf{0} \\
\end{array}
\rightarrow
\begin{array}{c}
\overset{1}{\mathbf{6}}2 \\
\times \mathbf{52} \\
\hline
124 \\
\mathbf{31}0 \\
\end{array}
\rightarrow
\begin{array}{c}
62 \\
\times 52 \\
\hline
124 \\
+310 \\
\hline
3,224 \\
\end{array}
$$

© Garlic Press Eugene, OR

| $\begin{array}{r}82\\ \times 64\end{array}$ | $\begin{array}{r}31\\ \times 85\end{array}$ | $\begin{array}{r}83\\ \times 73\end{array}$ | $\begin{array}{r}91\\ \times 47\end{array}$ | $\begin{array}{r}52\\ \times 52\end{array}$ | $\begin{array}{r}71\\ \times 69\end{array}$ | $\begin{array}{r}92\\ \times 93\end{array}$ | $\begin{array}{r}72\\ \times 34\end{array}$ |

| $\begin{array}{r}61\\ \times 28\end{array}$ | $\begin{array}{r}72\\ \times 92\end{array}$ | $\begin{array}{r}53\\ \times 42\end{array}$ | $\begin{array}{r}32\\ \times 54\end{array}$ | $\begin{array}{r}91\\ \times 89\end{array}$ | $\begin{array}{r}42\\ \times 73\end{array}$ | $\begin{array}{r}62\\ \times 22\end{array}$ | $\begin{array}{r}81\\ \times 57\end{array}$ |

| $\begin{array}{r}62\\ \times 34\end{array}$ | $\begin{array}{r}93\\ \times 93\end{array}$ | $\begin{array}{r}71\\ \times 84\end{array}$ | $\begin{array}{r}94\\ \times 42\end{array}$ | $\begin{array}{r}62\\ \times 73\end{array}$ | $\begin{array}{r}92\\ \times 92\end{array}$ | $\begin{array}{r}81\\ \times 79\end{array}$ | $\begin{array}{r}42\\ \times 54\end{array}$ |

| $\begin{array}{r}63\\ \times 73\end{array}$ | $\begin{array}{r}82\\ \times 93\end{array}$ | $\begin{array}{r}51\\ \times 64\end{array}$ | $\begin{array}{r}43\\ \times 43\end{array}$ | $\begin{array}{r}84\\ \times 62\end{array}$ | $\begin{array}{r}73\\ \times 83\end{array}$ | $\begin{array}{r}51\\ \times 26\end{array}$ | $\begin{array}{r}62\\ \times 82\end{array}$ |

NAME
NOMBRE _____

Instructions:

1. **Answer all the math problems first.**
2. **Cut out one puzzle piece at a time.**
3. **Paste the puzzle piece in the box with the same answer.**

Instrucciones:

1. Conteste todos los problemas de matemáticas primero.
2. Recorte una pieza del rompecabezas a la vez.
3. Pegue la pieza del rompecabezas en el recuadro que tiene la misma respuesta.

1,708	**4,526**	**5,208**	**1,364**
4,599	**2,226**	**6,399**	**2,108**
5,964	**1,326**	**3,264**	**8,099**

62
x22

91
x89
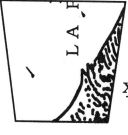

53
x42

61
x28
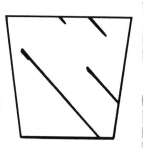

81
x79
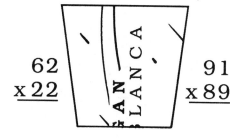

62
x73

71
x84

62
x34

51
x26

84
x62

51
x64

63
x73
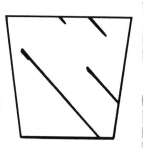

12

$$38 \rightarrow \overset{3}{3}8 \rightarrow \overset{3}{3}8 \rightarrow \overset{5}{\overset{\cancel{3}}{3}}8 \rightarrow \overset{5}{\overset{\cancel{3}}{3}}8 \rightarrow 38$$

$$\begin{array}{r} 38 \\ \times 74 \\ \hline \end{array} \rightarrow \begin{array}{r} \overset{3}{3}8 \\ \times 74 \\ \hline 2 \end{array} \rightarrow \begin{array}{r} \overset{3}{3}8 \\ \times 74 \\ \hline 152 \end{array} \rightarrow \begin{array}{r} \overset{5}{\cancel{3}}8 \\ \times 74 \\ \hline 152 \\ 60 \end{array} \rightarrow \begin{array}{r} \overset{5}{\cancel{3}}8 \\ \times 74 \\ \hline 152 \\ 2660 \end{array} \rightarrow \begin{array}{r} 38 \\ \times 74 \\ \hline {}^{1}152 \\ +2660 \\ \hline 2{,}812 \end{array}$$

75	63	28	54	48	92	37	27
x95	x67	x86	x79	x38	x96	x87	x89

84	97	54	76	32	65	73	27
x68	x72	x45	x66	x89	x53	x98	x47

59	98	74	49	95	62	89	56
x46	x79	x67	x33	x39	x86	x74	x35

78	46	97	83	36	58	72	44
x27	x88	x65	x99	x67	x23	x75	x69

NAME
NOMBRE _____

Instructions:

1. **Answer all the math problems first.**
2. **Cut out one puzzle piece at a time.**
3. **Paste the puzzle piece in the box with the same answer.**

Instrucciones:

1. Conteste todos los problemas de matemáticas primero.
2. Recorte una pieza del rompecabezas a la vez.
3. Pegue la pieza del rompecabezas en el recuadro que tiene la misma respuesta.

6,586	2,106	2,848	5,712
2,430	5,400	2,412	4,958
6,305	3,705	2,714	7,154

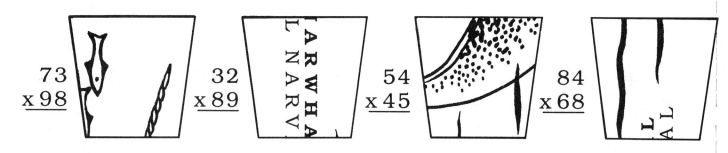

$$73 \times 98 \qquad 32 \times 89 \qquad 54 \times 45 \qquad 84 \times 68$$

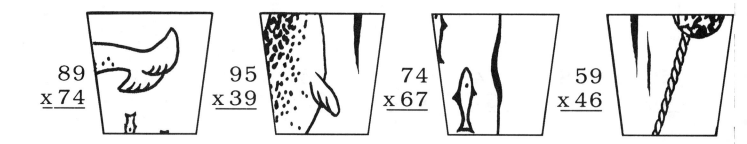

$$89 \times 74 \qquad 95 \times 39 \qquad 74 \times 67 \qquad 59 \times 46$$

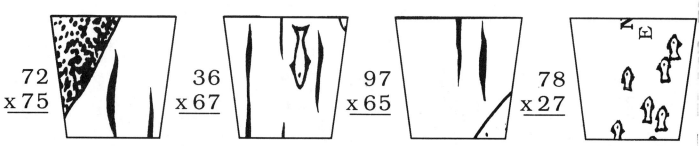

$$72 \times 75 \qquad 36 \times 67 \qquad 97 \times 65 \qquad 78 \times 27$$

14

$$
86 \rightarrow \begin{matrix} ^5 \\ 8\mathbf{6} \\ \times 4\mathbf{9} \\ \hline \mathbf{4} \end{matrix} \rightarrow \begin{matrix} ^5 \\ \mathbf{8}6 \\ \times 4\mathbf{9} \\ \hline \mathbf{7}\mathbf{7}4 \end{matrix} \rightarrow \begin{matrix} ^2 \\ 8\mathbf{6} \\ \times \mathbf{4}9 \\ \hline 774 \\ \mathbf{4}\bigcirc \end{matrix} \rightarrow \begin{matrix} ^2 \\ \mathbf{8}6 \\ \times \mathbf{4}9 \\ \hline 774 \\ \mathbf{34}4\bigcirc \end{matrix} \rightarrow \begin{matrix} 86 \\ \times 49 \\ \hline ^1 774 \\ +^1 344\bigcirc \\ \hline 4{,}214 \end{matrix}
$$

© Garlic Press Eugene, OR

63	28	54	49	58	95	89	23
x 97	x 86	x 79	x 36	x 64	x 97	x 42	x 98

56	73	48	92	34	87	75	68
x 36	x 94	x 38	x 86	x 47	x 59	x 25	x 34

39	77	86	29	95	67	98	85
x 35	x 86	x 48	x 46	x 56	x 47	x 94	x 33

32	57	94	36	97	58	82	56
x 86	x 23	x 45	x 84	x 78	x 26	x 67	x 35

NAME
NOMBRE _____

Instructions:

1. Answer <u>all</u> the math problems first.
2. Cut out <u>one</u> puzzle piece at a time.
3. Paste the puzzle piece in the box with the same answer.

Instrucciones:

1. Conteste <u>todos</u> los problemas de matemáticas primero.
2. Recorte <u>una</u> pieza del rompecabezas a la vez.
3. Pegue la pieza del rompecabezas en el recuadro que tiene la misma respuesta.

4,128	2,016	1,598	7,566
1,875	2,752	1,365	5,320
5,494	9,212	4,230	1,824

75
x25

34
x47

48
x38

56
x36

98
x94

95
x56

86
x48

39
x35

82
x67

97
x78

94
x45

32
x86

16

$$
\begin{array}{r}
395 \\
\times 46 \\
\hline
\end{array}
\rightarrow
\begin{array}{r}
5\ 3 \\
395 \\
\times 46 \\
\hline
2370 \\
\end{array}
\rightarrow
\begin{array}{r}
3\ 2 \\
\not{5}\ \not{3} \\
395 \\
\times 46 \\
\hline
2370 \\
1580\ 0 \\
\end{array}
\rightarrow
\begin{array}{r}
395 \\
\times 46 \\
\hline
^12370 \\
+1580\ 0 \\
\hline
18{,}170 \\
\end{array}
$$

© Garlic Press Eugene, OR

945	586	835	958	649	297	463	737
x67	x42	x94	x33	x79	x48	x89	x37

269	487	654	983	497	762	979	638
x76	x37	x48	x85	x44	x78	x69	x56

597	324	638	246	579	388	856	387
x83	x59	x38	x65	x92	x74	x36	x69

538	264	749	853	936	453	562	726
x65	x77	x84	x48	x97	x69	x85	x78

NAME
NOMBRE _____

Instructions:

1. Answer **all** the math problems first.
2. Cut out **one** puzzle piece at a time.
3. Paste the puzzle piece in the box with the same answer.

Instrucciones:

1. Conteste <u>todos</u> los problemas de matemáticas primero.
2. Recorte <u>una</u> pieza del rompecabezas a la vez.
3. Pegue la pieza del rompecabezas en el recuadro que tiene la misma respuesta.

20,444	**34,970**	**90,792**	**24,244**
67,551	**49,551**	**21,868**	**62,916**
53,268	**31,392**	**47,770**	**30,816**

979
x69

497
x44

654
x48

269
x76

856
x36

579
x92

638
x38

597
x83

562
x85

936
x97

749
x84

538
x65

18

```
                 5 2              5 2
    584    →     584    →    5̶2̶        584
   x76          x76          584   →   x76
               ────          x76      ¹3504
               3504         ────     +4088○
                           3504      ──────
                          4088○       44,384
```

© Garlic Press Eugene, OR

359	798	365	846	289	575	428	737
x43	x95	x49	x86	x57	x96	x78	x34

217	832	425	954	688	343	797	413
x58	x96	x85	x57	x89	x45	x62	x89

928	267	423	629	132	793	329	678
x94	x87	x75	x46	x99	x68	x79	x52

537	762	974	347	838	995	416	737
x43	x85	x39	x77	x53	x84	x48	x67

NAME
NOMBRE _____

Instructions:

1. **Answer <u>all</u> the math problems first.**
2. **Cut out <u>one</u> puzzle piece at a time.**
3. **Paste the puzzle piece in the box with the same answer.**

Instrucciones:

1. Conteste <u>todos</u> los problemas de matemáticas primero.
2. Recorte <u>una</u> pieza del rompecabezas a la vez.
3. Pegue la pieza del rompecabezas en el recuadro que tiene la misma respuesta.

87,232	**23,091**	**36,125**	**13,068**
19,968	**25,991**	**37,986**	**49,414**
61,232	**44,414**	**31,725**	**12,586**

797
x62

688
x89

425
x85

217
x58

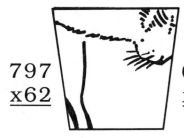

329
x79

132
x99

423
x75

928
x94

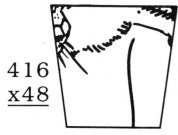

416
x48

838
x53

974
x39

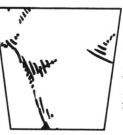

537
x43

ARCTIC HARE
LA LIEBRE ÁRTIC

© Garlic Press
Eugene, OR

```
        3 8        3 7
  739    739       ⅔⅝      739
 x89   x89       x89     x89
       ───────    ───────    ───────
       6651       6651     6651
                  5912○   ⁺5912○
                           ───────
                           65,771
```

739 → 739 → 739 → 739

© Garlic Press Eugene, OR

239	798	859	345	843	267	923	572
x69	x52	x32	x86	x95	x99	x98	x86

347	886	558	647	394	528	967	473
x64	x76	x39	x87	x35	x56	x72	x49

775	678	526	294	472	937	469	247
x47	x24	x65	x97	x88	x73	x96	x58

955	789	526	768	384	832	756	489
x75	x43	x87	x28	x79	x95	x68	x45

NAME
NOMBRE _____

Instructions:

1. Answer <u>all</u> the math problems first.
2. Cut out <u>one</u> puzzle piece at a time.
3. Paste the puzzle piece in the box with the same answer.

Instrucciones:

1. Conteste <u>todos</u> los problemas de matemáticas primero.
2. Recorte <u>una</u> pieza del rompecabezas a la vez.
3. Pegue la pieza del rompecabezas en el recuadro que tiene la misma respuesta.

69,624	45,762	36,425	45,024
41,536	30,336	71,625	51,408
21,762	34,190	13,790	22,208

967
x72

394
x35

558
x39

347
x64

469
x96

472
x88

526
x65

775
x47

756
x68

384
x79

526
x87

955
x75

$$
\begin{array}{r}
486 \\
\times 96 \\
\end{array}
\rightarrow
\begin{array}{r}
5\ 3 \\
486 \\
\times 96 \\
\hline
2916 \\
\end{array}
\rightarrow
\begin{array}{r}
7\ 5 \\
\cancel{5\ 3} \\
486 \\
\times 96 \\
\hline
2916 \\
4374\bigcirc \\
\end{array}
\rightarrow
\begin{array}{r}
486 \\
\times 96 \\
\hline
{}^{1}2916 \\
+4374\bigcirc \\
\hline
46{,}656 \\
\end{array}
$$

© Garlic Press Eugene, OR

942	365	898	654	969	572	749	225
x58	x84	x73	x37	x68	x85	x43	x95

736	958	569	987	335	623	378	829
x67	x76	x25	x97	x56	x98	x77	x59

495	646	869	557	794	286	967	373
x48	x56	x72	x23	x49	x55	x92	x69

857	624	369	595	836	675	462	797
x25	x78	x56	x62	x88	x43	x76	x87

NAME
NOMBRE _____

Instructions:

1. Answer <u>all</u> the math problems first.
2. Cut out <u>one</u> puzzle piece at a time.
3. Paste the puzzle piece in the box with the same answer.

Instrucciones:

1. Conteste <u>todos</u> los problemas de matemáticas primero.
2. Recorte <u>una</u> pieza del rompecabezas a la vez.
3. Pegue la pieza del rompecabezas en el recuadro que tiene la misma respuesta.

49,312	38,906	21,425	18,760
20,664	29,106	73,568	23,760
14,225	62,568	35,112	88,964

378
x77

335
x56

569
x25

736
x67

967
x92

794
x49

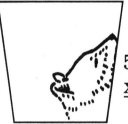
869
x72

495
x48

462
x76
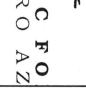
836
x88

369
x56

857
x25

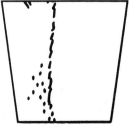

24

NAME
NOMBRE _____

$$
\begin{array}{r}
347 \\
\times\ 64 \\
\hline
^1 1388 \\
+\ 2082 \\
\hline
22,208
\end{array}
$$

○ 22,408
○ 22,228
● 22,208

$$
\begin{array}{r}
675 \\
\times\ 43 \\
\end{array}
$$
○ 29,025
○ 28,035
○ 29,035

$$
\begin{array}{r}
489 \\
\times\ 45 \\
\end{array}
$$
○ 21,005
○ 22,005
○ 22,055

$$
\begin{array}{r}
596 \\
\times\ 2 \\
\end{array}
$$
○ 1,189
○ 1,292
○ 1,192

$$
\begin{array}{r}
57 \\
\times\ 23 \\
\end{array}
$$
○ 1,311
○ 1,331
○ 3,311

$$
\begin{array}{r}
918 \\
\times\ 9 \\
\end{array}
$$
○ 8,272
○ 8,262
○ 8,622

$$
\begin{array}{r}
76 \\
\times\ 66 \\
\end{array}
$$
○ 5,016
○ 5,106
○ 5,006

$$
\begin{array}{r}
942 \\
\times\ 58 \\
\end{array}
$$
○ 52,636
○ 54,636
○ 54,366

$$
\begin{array}{r}
294 \\
\times\ 97 \\
\end{array}
$$
○ 26,518
○ 28,588
○ 28,518

$$
\begin{array}{r}
425 \\
\times\ 85 \\
\end{array}
$$
○ 36,125
○ 36,225
○ 38,125

$$
\begin{array}{r}
324 \\
\times\ 59 \\
\end{array}
$$
○ 19,166
○ 19,116
○ 18,166

$$
\begin{array}{r}
49 \\
\times\ 36 \\
\end{array}
$$
○ 1,764
○ 1,864
○ 1,774

$$
\begin{array}{r}
934 \\
\times\ 8 \\
\end{array}
$$
○ 7,742
○ 7,272
○ 7,472

$$
\begin{array}{r}
97 \\
\times\ 72 \\
\end{array}
$$
○ 6,894
○ 6,984
○ 6,994

$$
\begin{array}{r}
736 \\
\times\ 5 \\
\end{array}
$$
○ 3,880
○ 3,660
○ 3,680

$$
\begin{array}{r}
267 \\
\times\ 87 \\
\end{array}
$$
○ 23,209
○ 23,229
○ 24,229

$$
\begin{array}{r}
832 \\
\times\ 95 \\
\end{array}
$$
○ 79,440
○ 78,040
○ 79,040

$$
\begin{array}{r}
624 \\
\times\ 78 \\
\end{array}
$$
○ 49,672
○ 48,672
○ 48,622

$$
\begin{array}{r}
586 \\
\times\ 42 \\
\end{array}
$$
○ 24,612
○ 26,412
○ 24,662

Answers
Lessons 1 -12 & Post-Test

Page 1.

38	72	64	90	56	84	96	74
54	98	75	56	92	84	70	75
96	85	50	87	68	90	76	81
72	95	78	60	94	91	45	52

Page 3.

675	136	581	280	744	188	516	237
108	264	340	432	216	195	392	873
272	329	558	162	435	378	784	144
265	774	476	300	114	632	570	207

Page 5.

4,375	1,398	3,300	5,243	8,586	2,964	1,095	4,584
3,894	2,271	8,415	3,536	6,128	1,750	2,572	1,335
1,716	5,247	3,372	4,944	3,516	5,562	1,240	2,808
1,728	3,680	6,594	1,158	2,140	8,262	3,915	5,176

Page 7.

4,338	1,568	1,044	4,815	1,154	3,537	7,584	1,730
1,404	5,211	2,190	2,841	1,188	3,816	2,772	3,470
2,625	6,714	1,388	7,936	1,225	3,412	6,516	1,264
7,472	1,192	2,290	5,719	8,604	4,098	6,616	4,543

Page 9.

903	726	869	506	825	713	528	836
714	913	504	968	616	902	814	529
308	416	759	924	408	935	736	517
946	737	704	516	858	715	429	748

Page 11.

5,248	2,635	6,059	4,277	2,704	4,899	8,556	2,448
1,708	6,624	2,226	1,728	8,099	3,066	1,364	4,617
2,108	8,649	5,964	3,948	4,526	8,464	6,399	2,268
4,599	7,626	3,264	1,849	5,208	6,059	1,326	5,084

Page 13.

7,125	4,221	2,408	4,266	1,824	8,832	3,219	2,403
5,712	6,984	2,430	5,016	2,848	3,445	7,154	1,269
2,714	7,742	4,958	1,617	3,705	5,332	6,586	1,960
2,106	4,048	6,305	8,217	2,412	1,334	5,400	3,036

Page 15.

6,111	2,408	4,266	1,764	3,712	9,215	3,738	2,254
2,016	6,862	1,824	7,912	1,598	5,133	1,875	2,312
1,365	6,622	4,128	1,334	5,320	3,149	9,212	2,805
2,752	1,311	4,230	3,024	7,566	1,508	5,494	1,960

Page 17.

63,315	24,612	78,490	31,614	51,271	14,256	41,207	27,269
20,444	18,019	31,392	83,555	21,868	59,436	67,551	35,728
49,551	19,116	24,244	15,990	53,268	28,712	30,816	26,703
34,970	20,328	62,916	40,944	90,792	31,257	47,770	56,628

Page 19.

15,437	75,810	17,885	72,756	16,473	55,200	33,384	25,058
12,586	79,872	36,125	54,378	61,232	15,435	49,414	36,757
87,232	23,229	31,725	28,934	13,068	53,924	25,991	35,256
23,091	64,770	37,986	26,719	44,414	83,580	19,968	49,379

Page 21.

16,491	41,496	27,488	29,670	80,085	26,433	90,454	49,192
22,208	67,336	21,762	56,289	13,790	29,568	69,624	23,177
36,425	16,272	34,190	28,518	41,536	68,401	45,024	14,326
71,625	33,927	45,762	21,504	30,336	79,040	51,408	22,005

Page 23.

54,636	30,660	65,554	24,198	65,892	48,620	32,207	21,375
49,312	72,808	14,225	95,739	18,760	61,054	29,106	48,911
23,760	36,176	62,568	12,811	38,906	15,730	88,964	25,737
21,425	48,672	20,664	36,890	73,568	29,025	35,112	69,339

Page 25-Post Test.

	22,208	29,025	22,005
1,192	1,311	8,262	5,016
54,636	28,518	36,125	19,116
1,764	7,472	6,984	3,680
23,229	79,040	48,672	24,612

Polar Bear

The polar bear is found in the Arctic. It moves through snow, across ice floes and swims in search of seals, birds, fish, and vegetation.

El Oso Polar

El oso polar se encuentra en el Artico. Se mueve por la nieve, a través del hielo flotante, y nada en busca de focas, aves, peces y vegetación.

Musk Ox

The musk ox is found in the Arctic. Musk oxen feed from the tundra in summer and from mosses and lichens hidden beneath the snow in winter. They huddle together for protection and warmth.

La Cabra de Almizcle

La cabra de almizcle se encuentra en el Artico. Las cabras de almizcle se alimentan de la tundra en verano y de los musgos y líquenes escondidos debajo de la nieve en invierno. Se acurrucan juntas para protección y calor.

Caribou

The caribou are found in the Arctic. They migrate on the tundra in search of food during the summer, heading south to forest areas in winter. Caribou are also called reindeer.

El Caribú

El caribú se encuentra en las orillas del Artico. Durante el verano, emigran sobre la tundra en busca de alimento, regresando a los bosques del sur en invierno. También al caribú se le conoce por el nombre de reno.

Puffin

Puffin live in northern ocean waters. They live in colonies and nest in burrows along ocean cliffs. They are better swimmers and divers than fliers.

El Frailecillo

Los frailecillos habitan en las aguas oceánicas del norte. Viven en colonias y se anidan en madigueras construidas en las rocas de los precipicios a la orilla del mar. Son mejores nadadores y buceadores que voladores.

Arctic Tern

The arctic tern flies from Arctic to Antarctic and back again each year (40,000 km or 25,000 miles). Terns have two summers. When winter comes to the Arctic, they fly to the Antarctic. When it is winter in the Antarctic, they fly to the Arctic.

La Golondrina de Mar

Cada año la golondrina de mar vuela del Artico a la Antártica de ida y vuelta(40,000 km o 25,000 millas). Así las golondrinas de mar gozan de dos veranos. Cuando llega el invierno al Artico, vuelan a la Antártica. Cuando es invierno en la Antártica, vuelan al Artico.

Ptarmigan

The ptarmigan is found on all continents circling the Arctic. It follows the receding snow in summer, feeding on berries, buds and insects. In winter it returns south into protected areas.

La Perdiz Blanca

La perdiz blanca se encuentra en todos los continentes alrededor del Artico. Sigue el retroceder de la nieve en verano, alimentándose de bayas, brotes e insectos. En invierno regresa al sur a las zonas protegidas.

Narwhal

The narwhal is found in Antarctic waters. Males, and some females, have a spiral tooth which grows up to 8 feet (2.5 m).

El Narval

El narval se encuentra en las aguas de la Antártica. Los machos, y algunas hembras también, tienen un diente espiral que se prolonga hasta cerca de 8 pies (2.5m).

Walrus

Walrus are found in Arctic waters. They live in herds on rocks and islands. They feed on crabs and clams. They are a close relative of the seal.

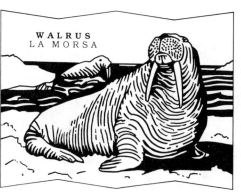

La Morsa

Las morsas se encuentran en las aguas del Artico. Viven en manadas sobre las rocas e islas. Se alimentan de cangrejos y almejas. Son parientes de la foca.